a canoe in midstream

a canoe in midstream
poems new & old

APIRANA TAYLOR

Canterbury University Press

First published in 2009 by
CANTERBURY UNIVERSITY PRESS
University of Canterbury
Private Bag 4800, Christchurch
NEW ZEALAND
www.canterbury.ac.nz/engage/cup
Reprinted 2019

Text copyright © 2009 Apirana Taylor

The moral rights of the author have been asserted.
ISBN 978-1-877257-79-7

A catalogue record for this book is available from the
National Library of New Zealand.

Design and pre-press production by Rachel Scott
Cover painting by Apirana Taylor
Author photograph by Himiona Grace
Printed by Your Books, Wellington

these verses are paddles
to the waka
a canoe of poems
in midstream

i dedicate this book
to my darling Pru
our beautiful children
and whanau

I would like to acknowledge the assistance
of Te Waka Toi, which enabled me to work on the
manuscript and write many of the later poems in
this book. I am also grateful to Canterbury
University Press for their continued support.

Apirana Taylor

Contents

Intro   11
Te Kooti   12
The Womb   13
Taiaha Haka Poem   14
A Departure   15
Sad Joke on a Marae   16
Moon Magic   17
The Pohangina Hawk   18
The Seagull   19
Evil Winds   20
In the Heartbeat   21
Thoughts on the Road   22
Leap Frog   23
Patu Pounamu   24
Thunder God   25
Spring   26
The Puriri Tree   27
A Man   28
Whakapapa   29
I Am   30
Te Ihi   31
Ki a Pru   32
The Family Tree   33
Listen   34
Weaving   35
Carving   36
Rite Tonu   37
Uncle Hakaraia   38
Grrrrrrr   39
Nga Kahu   41
New Hawks   42
The Mushroom   43
Soft Leaf Falls of Light   44
The Moon   45

Gold   46
Play time   47
How Great   49
Maori Girl   50
K Mart way   51
Guts   52
To my darling Pru   53
searching   54
seeking   54
looking   54
huri huri   55
Kapiti   56
Titoko   59
Parihaka   60
before the mountain   62
zigzag roads   63
fishbone   64
Lady Anorexia   65
breaking through   66
Hinemoa's daughter   67
understanding   68
aids   69
nature calls   70
on Paekakariki Beach   71
the temple   72
Rawene   73
startled birds   74
we are   75
my whenua   75
close   77
haka   78
the worm   79
Coca-Cola Jesus and Mitsubishi Mary   80
tangiwai   81
poem for a princess   82
dole-day warrior   83
e Api e   84
harakeke   85

to Te Rerenga Wairua   86
it is   87
time (1), time (2), time (3)   88
thought   89
struck   90
invisible   91
a great seamstress   92
Swiss mountains   93
survivor   94
stone age   95
aroha   96
the heavenly miracle   97
autumn (1), autumn (2)   98
blood drops   99
the Sami   100
the bellow   101
He Dog   102
warriors of love   103
dragons   104
the bomber   105
Easter eggs   106
six million   107
peace lanterns   108
in the wind   110
Charteris Bay   112
the mauri   113
rules   114
comfort   115
walls of the night   116
Golden Bay   117
teardrop   118
painter   119
te ata kura   120
Darts   121
a sprig of beech   122
cold   123
all saints day   124
senyru   125

little tea cups   126
the swamp   127
the wolf   128
the feral cat   129
the dream is real   130
kete   131
free   133
pepetuna   134
the rose of peace   135
a line dropped from heaven   136
jetty in the night   137
stance   138
4 lingual poem   139
what i am   140
words   141
rat a tat tat   142
water   144
questioning   145
catching the waka   146
can u c   149
fisherman's platter   150
animal   151
(to Pru)   152
Pru   153
O sun   154
Daughter   154
Reremoana   154
Growing   155
flight   156
sipping   157
time to leave   158
atea   159
poem to Hone Tuwhare   160
Thoughts before the headstone 08   161
WAITANGI   163
as if asleep   164
Tiki tiki   165
forever   166
whew   167

Intro

Handle with care.
Skim my paper sails.
Read me again.
Unfurl and let
the winds of poetry blow

Te Kooti

Once hangi grew
like melon pregnant bellies
full of black and white flesh.

Now the stones are cold.
Te Kooti is dead
under incubus earth.

We are ashes of his fire
dead a hundred years.

Safe in our houses
we have stripped him
to a feather in the wind
as distant as a morepork
that calls in the night.

The Womb

Your fires burnt my forests
leaving only the charred bones
of totara rimu and kahikatea.

Your ploughs like the fingernails
of a woman scarred my face.
It seems I became a domestic giant.

But in death
you settlers and farmers
return to me
and I suck on your bodies
as if they are lollipops.

I am the land
the womb of life and death.
Ruamoko the unborn God
rumbles within me
and the fires of Ruapehu still live.

Taiaha Haka Poem

I am Te – ngau – reka - a – tu
I once danced with killers
who followed the war god
beyond the gates of hell
to kill in the gardens of pleasure.

I am the taiaha left among people
who dance and twirl poi
in gaudy halls
of plastic Maoridom.

Father give me guts.
War god why
have you forsaken me?

A Departure

The sea lashed rocks
like broken teeth
where alone he stood
with waves crashing
the song of time's whiplash tongue.

Alone on the beach
he watched the sun
plunge into the sea.
And felt his life
like a river bleed dry.

He saw a fish
stripped tossed and speared
by the beak
of a flesh-gobbling gull.

His mind snapped.
His heart thumped memories
from the spring of his days.

Then later in the morning light
with the sun
flung skywards from the sea
he visioned life and death
bodylocked like Siamese twins.

He saw an island born
to the storm's swirl and thrust
and felt the ocean suck the marrow
from his mountain bones.
And without fear
he released eighty years
to the outgoing tide
for he understood
his journey uncurled
the fish the sea
the island and the sun.

Sad Joke on a Marae

Tihei Mauriora I called
Kupe Paikea Te Kooti
Rewi and Te Rauparaha.
I saw them
grim death and wooden ghosts
carved on the meeting house wall.

In the only Maori I knew
I called
Tihei Mauriora.
Above me the tekoteko raged.
He ripped his tongue from his mouth
and threw it at my feet.

Then I spoke.
My name is Tu the freezing worker.
Ngati D.B. is my tribe.
The pub is my Marae.
My fist is my taiaha.
Jail is my home.

Tihei Mauriora I cried.
They understood
the tekoteko and the ghosts
though I said nothing but
Tihei Mauriora
for that's all I knew.

Moon Magic

Ah that moon magic
twisting the skulls
of poets lovers
and pagan priests.

Lend me the moon's eyes
and I'll die tomorrow
having lived
a thousand years.

The Pohangina Hawk

Up Pohangina flies a hawk.
Above the valley it soars
with blood-red talons
it grips a mouse
and holds the world in its claws

This is the hawk
that rips the meat
from hills older
than the forgotten hour.

From a living mouse
it strips the flesh
till heart and gut are exposed.
Then away it glides
across the land
and ageless mountain bones.

The Seagull

He flew high above the sea.
Within the circle of his arms
the world was small.
Horizon to horizon
all oceans yielded to his beak.
Now the hourglass turns.
His wings clipped by hands of time.
He awaits winds that will not blow.
Waves wash over him.
Add salt to his body.
The sea comes hungry to the shore.
And he is a morsel on a table of sand.

Evil Winds

Rangi has been separated from Papa.
Yet even in winter, the coldest season of his
love,
his rays embrace earth.
Why are we not the same?
Alone in bed.
You are not by my side.

Ripped apart by drunken winds of rage
we have been hurled
further than the gods.
If only I had the sun's arms
I would reach out
and hold you again.

In the Heartbeat

Little canary
you
have broken
the bars
of
life's cage.

Beauty lives.
Even in the
heartbeat
of death.

Thoughts on the Road

See how the twin peaks rise
under the hands of the sun's warm rays.
And the arms of the rainbow
that embrace the earth
in moist lovemaking.

Lost in creation they are undisturbed
by my presence
for I am from them.

Skyfather Earthmother
the old people were right.
I see the union
of sun and earth
and hear their songs of fertility.

Leap Frog

This pond
like
a mirror
reflects
the sky.

A frog breaks the surface
leaps high
above the sun
and falls
back into
a sea of clouds.

Patu Pounamu

This is the haka of the patu pounamu

that in the veins of the race of the flicking tongue

and rolling eye

warms to the beat of the feet thumping the earth

in the rhythm of war

Thunder God

Over the dark sky I gather

lightning lives within me

the clouds are my cloak

hear my pain see my anger feel my power

beware

I am the thunder god

Spring

Spring

where do you come from?
where do you go?

I am like a bud
on a tree

that will live, wither
and never know

The Puriri Tree

See how the young puriri tree grows
as with tender leaves
he licks the sky

to me
the birth of all that seeks life
is like this puriri tree

surrounded by death's darkness
reaching beyond the night

as with hope newly born
on each delicate stem

he fights each day for life

A Man

Two eyes

one mind

so proud

so blind

I am a man

Whakapapa

For too long now he'd sought his whakapapa
sought and unfound whakapapa
whirled in the wind
whistled in the leaves
first there was Rangi and Papa
that was the first whakapapa, or was that Te Kore?
Then there was dark and light, night and day.
What was that whakapapa?
And all the different kinds of dark and light
the light turning the world turning
the night the long night
whakapapa whakapapa
who was he? He began again
the moko on the chief's face
or those strong enough to take it is whakapapa
the mauri, eternal life force
tihei that's the sneeze
tihei tihei tihei
whakapapa whakapapa ties you to the land
the ropes are cut – what did he inherit?
Dole queues longer than your arm
uneducated unmotivated unqualified, drunk again
of neither this world nor the other
so Rangi the skyfather and Papatuanuku the earthmother
lay together in love's embrace
the gods were born
and then remember Maui
Maui Maui Maui and Tawhaki climbing the vine
and the marae, whakapiri tonu, whakapiri tonu
there is more much more
lift yourself up boy
where the flowers grow is the whakapapa of light
where the flowers sleep is the whakapapa of darkness
you are Ngati
this is your inheritance
the sky and earth and all that lies between.

I Am

My heart is creation
my bones are destruction
my feet are screams
they walk and run to
the rhythm and chatter of bullets
my eyes are wings
they cross mountains and seas
I'm a killer who weeps for the poor
I love humanity and bathe you in gore
I am rightly wrong and wrongly right
I am lovers' freedom
I am loved and cherished
I am feared and hated
I raise governments
and destroy them
I am time's earthquake
and the rising sun
I'm anti-oppression
when it's wrong
I'm pro-oppression
when it's right
I hunger for change
I am sanity and madness
never satisfied
I am you
I thirst for the waters of knowledge
and I burn
I burn and I burn and I burn
in the streets
in your hearts and minds
I am fire
I am revolution

Te Ihi

From where does it come, te ha
the life breath
and what strange winds blow
through this house
in the drift and flow
of whaikorero
the call
ka ea ka ea
it is clear, it is clear
whakapiri tonu whakapiri tonu
hold fast, hold fast to what
te ihi, te ihi, te ihi
te ihi, what is that
te ihi, what is this word
te ihi, te ihi, what is it
kia mau, kia mau ki te aha
he paua mura ahi nga kanohi o Tumatauenga
the flashing eyes of Tu
haka it is haka
lightning flashing in the sky
rapa rapa te uira
ka tangi te whatitiri
and thunder
the beat of the feet till the earth shakes
kia whakatahoki au i a au
from where does it come, te ha
the life breath, te ihi
the sobbing wailing and laughter

Ki a Pru

I te po, i te pouri

Ka huri au ki a koe

Te whaea o aku tamariki

te manawa o te iwi

The Family Tree

I was
am
and will be

alive
growing
bearing fruit

living
dying
in you
and me

I am
the
family tree

Listen

Listen to the tap tap tap
of the carvers
as with chisel and mallet
they trace their genealogy
each to their own source turns
to the rhythmic flow
of spiral to
the inland fern
to the curl of waves
in the deep sea
listen with your eyes
see with your ears
the story learnt remembered and retold
in reaching back
to the living now
and of days to come
tap tap tap
through the window
there comes a light
a time of seeking
losing finding and creating

Weaving

From harakeke to kit
a lot of work
desire of heart and mind
make light of it
plait deftly the flax
follow the tradition of your ancestors
weave in yourself of yourself
life anew
with patterns handed down
and passed on
and new designs
of this world
so old and new
flow together
beautiful as kowhaiwhai
weave a kit in remembrance of Tane
who gained the kits of knowledge
silently weave this kit
tell all the stories
for those of us who have lost the art

Carving

With chisel and mallet
shape the wood
till out of kauri
emerges a figure
go deep to get
the right shape
go too deep
and you lose it all
find the grain
follow it
as the heartwood yields
to your chisel
body arms legs all one
proportion must be right
here is the spiral
like the punga and rolling waves
pause a moment
cease tap tap tap
brush away waste wood
chips and shavings
you've no time for that
you carve life

Rite Tonu

Rite tonu te ahua

HOW

o taku ngakau

MUCH

ki te moana

DO

e papaki ana

WE

ki nga toka

UNDERSTAND?

tangi

tangi

e

Uncle Hakaraia

Uncle Hakaraia Taurima
spoke no English till he went to school
where because he spoke Maori only
he was stood in the corner and made to feel
like a dumbcluck and a fool
you're here to learn English said the teacher
that is what you will speak
it was hard trying not to speak Maori
the first time he forgot
crack the teacher belted his knuckles
with the edge of her ruler
Uncle Hakaraia learnt school was cruel
at school it was talk English or else
English Pakeha he got confused
English English English
he tried hard to be English for fifty years
something snapped like crying in his soul
he knows deep down his wairua is Maori
he speaks impeccable English
and can hardly string two or three words
of his Maori tongue together
when he speaks of school days
his language is bitter

Grrrrrrr

A great way
to build up
physique
muscles flexed
against blue sky
in early spring
so as to let in the sea

the rrrrrrr
of chainsaw
swung
criss cross
through the air
chopping off
each
limb
of
pohutukawa
grrrrrrr
not
killing
but thinning out the
tree

later
with more chainsaw
and a sharp axe
cutting up
the branches of that tree
firewood for winter
happiness no waste
I saw the deep red
in the heart and blood
of that tree
the blood of a rangatira

I felt the tree
was bleeding
I knew it
so I stopped
for I felt the need
to utter
a
karakia

Nga Kahu

I saw the hawks
circle in the air
on the wing high
they swooped
circled
a disc side arked
in the sky
the world
beneath
on the hunt together
the earth divided
into a grid
a pattern to track
the rat
and swoop
now wings
spread at ease
masters supreme
riding on the wind
over the horizon
and valleyed hills gliding
and gone

New Hawks

Hawks of a new age
sweep the sky
black triangled
metal winged
eyes a-glimmer
that precise grid pattern
the eggs waiting
to be
laid
the computer eye
scans
these masters returning
in
the morning light

The Mushroom

This beautiful mushroom
a red
flash
rising
in
majestic
slow
motion
choking
the
flowers
swallowing the
sun

I remember another time
little
mushrooms in a circle around
which the fairies danced

but this mushroom
growing
blossoming
petals of red blood towers
above
us all
soon there will be no more war
the talking will end

Soft Leaf Falls of Light

Soft leaf falls of light
soft light falls of leaf
leaf soft light falls
light soft leaf falls
light falls leaf soft
light light light
soft leaf falls of light

The Moon

Many faces has the moon
round and full as the O
or like a sliced peach or a banana
men have landed on it
but it can still look like a yellow balloon
or a canoe sailing across the seas of heaven
sometimes the moon has no face at all
that's the darkest hour
but always the moon returns
sometimes as a thin barely visible
fingernail grin
or a monarch or god
seated on a throne of clouds
looking down on a dark world
giving that luminous light
strange and bewitching
more suitable for ghosts wolf howls and
vampires
gods so old their names are forgotten
bathe in the fountains of the moon
and are made young again
lovers swear by it
to the Maori the moon is Hina
to others Sina the silver one
of the silver stone the silver god and silver
water
the moon it is said controls the menses
this could be true
for even the mighty sea itself
is dragged to and fro across the earth by
the moon
and the waves bow down and dash them-
selves
again and again upon the shore
according to the whim of the moon

Gold

Do not live
merely for gold

time turns
the body old

all value is lost
when the metal is sold

Play time

Neither girls
nor yet women they came
friends together
to the place where I'd hoped no one would come
because the sun felt good alone

perhaps it was this reason
brought them here wishing I was not here
an old man in a tattered coat busting up
their afternoon time together as they mine

so quietly they walked to the swings
and sat there not speaking at all

I looked away cause the afternoon sun warmed me
and the light that shone without
filled me like my soul was
a solar battery drinking up the light
I thought of a lizard basking in the sun
felt many lizards move in me
awaken and dream a good dream

awoke to the creak of unoiled cotterpins
they'd begun to swing
to play as almost always they'd done
now serious yet lazily swinging to and fro

I knew time played as they swung
backwards and forwards
between girl woman time
then out of time they moved apart
woman to girl girl to woman
together again in mid-swing
then more effort
hair wind trailing

good as flying and freedom
they stopped
as though they'd forgotten.
It'd never happen again I knew

but as I played with my son in the sun
one night later
I saw them again
seated on the swings
they began to swing to and fro
beneath the sun in the late afternoon

How Great

How great is love
J.C. was nailed up
and wore a crown of thorns
for love

soldiers in their graves
died for love

in each second of day
and night
a shot is fired
a victim bled for love

Maori Girl

Day begun
under the sun
walking to the shop
Maori girl
the day is not long
whistling a smile and, 'kia ora',
oh Polynesian beauty
stepping out of a Kahukiwa painting
so strong, Maori girl
the day is not long
with kids and shopping
housework and
no money
you're tops at kapa haka
you're learning te reo
picking yourself up
daughter of the race who knew
only too well
the moko of your whakapapa
mother to be
the ghosts of your ancestors tap on your
shoulders
the day is not long

K Mart way

I saw her today
walking through K Mart
with a vacant look
on her old leathered face
just thirty-two
she sat down by the fountain
not knowing why
she was there
her kid ran about
all amok
her husband beat her
she always takes him back
for a rerun
the bruises have gone down
but they never go
she's come out
to sit behind the shades in solitude
amid shoppers
promises of freedom
echoed in reflections of her plastic
K Mart sunglasses
the scars of her beatings
almost hidden
beneath her torn skin

Guts

I have eaten the heart
and intestine
of my enemies
I have drunk their blood
I have supped on their kidneys
with relish
I have swallowed their livers
fresh raw and bloody
I have shared the guts of my enemy
with my friends
vengeance is mine
my enemy is no more
my mana is great
I am loved by my people
and feared by many
I have tasted with delight
the food of chiefs
I am Te Rauparaha

To my darling Pru

Love

I love you
you I love
love you I
love I you
you love I
I love you

searching

thirty years' struggle
to unscramble my brain
trying to write this

yrteop
oetryp
etrypo
trypoe
rypoet
ypoetr

seeking

seeking the great poem
i write all day
leaving only this

"~"~;"

mouse droppings
on a page

looking

like a black eel
the Otakaro wends its way
under the archways of trees

ducks swim happily upstream
sailboat leaves float downstream

looking for answers

honeysuckle and agapanthus
are reflected in the dark water

beauty needs no reason to be

huri huri

huri huri turn turn
turn turn wiri wiri
huri huri huri huri
wiri wiri turn turn
the wind blows
wiri wiri blows
the wind huri
huri wiri wiri turn
turn the leaves
fall turn turn
huri huri wiri wiri

Kapiti

Kapiti
isle of chiefs
lies off the coast
of my eye
where Te Rauparaha ruled
in days gone by
ae Te Rauparaha
who cast his eye
over that southern sea
and took the trail
the bloody path of war
to conquer
as none before
oh bathed the country
in blood did he
feasted on the bones
of his enemy
when his canoes
took to the sea
butchered Tamaeharanui
for his treachery
many great ariki and rangatira
lined his belly
aaa the feasting that was done
to the thunder of haka
under the sun
and the lightning crack
of the musket
the Pakeha gun
and above it all the call of Te Rauparaha
aaa ha haaa

he passed like the wind
over the land
and all felt his breath

aaa Te Rauparaha
what times eh
out on the sea
the sailing ships sailing
whalers traders
times changing
like the troublesome winds
in the straights of Raukawa
that crafty man Grey
appealed to the old serpent's vanity
pulled his tooth
took him away across the sea
the politics and the dealings of Te Rauparaha
he settled almost every score
he made his enemy no more
now he himself
is no more
death swallows us all
where did such ambition lead?
you who drenched the sea
red with blood
your beloved son slain
aaa the price of war
the bones of warriors
piled high on the shore
washed away by a thousand
ebbs and flows of the tide

Te Rauparaha is dead
Te Rauparaha is dead
Te Rauparaha lives
in the back of my head

Te Rauparaha Te Rauparaha
beloved of your people
the mighty Ngati Toa
as you loved them

in peace and war
why did you not tend
the kumara gardens in peace?
You who took war's bloody path
you gained more
than even you saw
in your schemes and dreams
and lost it all
in a rain of blood

Titoko

whakapapa line of your
eternal genealogy like
lush tendrils
of the gourd spread across
the belly of Ranginui
flowering across the sky
like kowhaiwhai
you were a leaf of the clan
from the hapu
Ngati Manuhiakai
of the mighty Ngati Ruanui
child of Turi
seed of Aotea
a stem rising from
the offshoots
of Ngati Ruahine
Tangahoe and Nga Rauru
mighty in battle strong in peace
you fought for your people
the land shook
to your name
Titokowaru! Titokowaru!

Parihaka

we never knew
about Parihaka
it was never
taught anywhere
except maybe
around the fires
of Parihaka
itself at night
when stories
are told
of the soldiers
who came
with guns
to haul us up
by the roots
like trees
from our land
though the prophets
called peace peace
it was never
taught at school
it was all hushed up
how we listened
to the prophets
Tohu, Te Whiti
who called peace 'Rire rire
Paimarire'
but the only
peace the soldiers
knew
spoke through
the barrels
of their guns
threatening
our women children

it was never
taught or spoken
how we
were shackled
led away to the caves
and imprisoned
for ploughing our land

before the mountain

iiiiiiiiiiiiiiiiiiiiiiiiiiiiiiiiiiiiiiiiiiii

soldiers

come
at Parihaka
we sit

&&&&&&&&&&&

men women children
before the mountain

^

in peace

+

the soldiers

iiiiiiiiiiiiiiiiiiiiiiiiiiiiiiiiiiiiiiiiii
iiiiiiiiiiiiiiiiiiiiiiiiiiiiiiiiiiiiiiiiii
iiiiiiiiiiiiiiiiiiiiiiiiiiiiiiiiiiiiiiiiii

row upon
row upon
row upon
row

come to take us away
to tear us from the land
we the people
of the prophets
Te Whiti and Tohu
who sat

&&&&&&&&&&&&&&&&&&&

before the mountain
in peace

+

zigzag roads

roads in Taranaki
zigzag and snake their way
over the bitter earth
they seldom run straight

roadmakers
paid compensation
only when they ran the roads
through Pakeha land

they didn't have to pay
if they pushed their roads
through the tattered remnants
of Maori land

hence roads crazily
snake and zigzag
through the province

the liars' road
is never straight

fishbone

how it must've stuck in their gullets like a fishbone
to have their plans foiled by a black little one-eyed
monkey called Titokowaru

he could count his fighting warriors
on his fingers and toes
if he counted old women and children

Cameron gutted Taranaki
opened it up like a can of beans

he knew the cause was unjust

in search of honour glory riches and fame
they came Whitmore, McDonnell, von Tempsky
the Kai Iwi cavalry

their dreams lie buried on the battlefield

a bullet shot von Tempsky

he got a street named after him

Maxwell, his sabre thirsting for the blood of more
children, was shot on his horse charging again

blood and butchery

Whitmore, McDonnell, got hollow victory
meaningless medals empty fame

Titoko's army, old men, women, warriors and children
unbeaten, melted away, a fight over a woman they say
breaking of tapu
eat the rocks, chew and choke on the bones
sings Titokowaru jailed in his cave

Lady Anorexia

sister, thou dost not need make-up
thou art already well made
by thy maker
thy lips are beauty as they are
as art thou more beautiful than the heart can tell
thy body and thy soul
are gifts to be praised and loved
thou art special
there is no other like thee
thy body is thy house
to tend and care for
thy soul is a singing bird
let it sing
listen not to those who say
thou must be thin
or thou must be fat
thou must be this or that
or thou must have blonde hair
blue eyes a heart-shaped arse
and tits like a cow
but small dreams are these
of small men with small fantasies
smash the chains
they make for thee
the rich cat grows fat
whilst thou grow thinner than air
eat and be well
as thy maker loves thee
and intended thee to be

breaking through

the tiki hangs from her neck
on a thread of flax
the fetus of pounamu
lies tangled in her hair
above her heart

the planes fly around
the tangle of feet
the trample of sound
on concrete
the toot of cars
fills the city air

we live in another time

in this
supermarket of hate
she wears the moko
you can see it
beneath the scars on her chin

greenstone tears hang
from her ears

my sister breaks through

flowing from her wairua

crammed with the taonga
of her tipuna

Hinemoa's daughter

her hair is so long
you could plait it all the way to the moon
and weave it with a sprinkling of stars

she writes poetry
as only the muse can write

when she smiles
she melts the heart of God

'I'm from Te Arawa,' she says

she shows me her litany of scars
they climb like ladders
up the insides of her wrists

deep savage cuts to the bone
speak of her youth and the countless times
she sent herself along the path of the spirits
and sought the solace of Hine-nui-te-po

like her tipuna Hinemoa
she swam the lake
but her lake was of fire and death
broken bottles drunken fights
smashed families shattered and scattered whanau

and she made it
she crossed the troubled water
and found her tane who loves her
more deeply than the heart can tell

in the lost city
they raise many fine children
with aroha

understanding

understanding grows out of healing
healing grows out of life
life grows out of pain
pain grows out of feeling
fear grows out of not knowing
light grows out of knowing
healing grows out of understanding
love

aids

       aids
       aids
       aids
aids aids aids aids aids
aids aids aids aids aids
       aids
       aids
       aids
       aids
       aids
       aids

       help

nature calls

today God paints
daps of cloud over Paekakariki

sprinkles light misty rain
over Kapiti

a warm sun
sinks beneath the horizon

nature calls me to worship
in her temple

where I can feel the mauri
and breathe

on Paekakariki Beach

night

like a watercolour print

with a smudge of misty cloud

soft rain falls

lines of waves
trail like ribbons into the darkness

around the throat
of the sea

the lights of Pukerua Bay
and Raumati

burn like cigarette stubs

'we've had two youth suicides,' she says

there is meaning here

moonlit leaves lap the wind

the temple

to get the monkey off his back
he pays her fool's gold
she says that's all she wanted

hidden in the heart
beneath the sleaze make-up
and dollar bill
they seek true love

she spreads her legs like a fan
he grunts, she groans in false ecstasy
bed springs creak

his river flows
between her overworked thighs

'nothing like a night out whoring,'
he says as he leaves
choking on the ashes of distaste in his
mouth

she closes the door
thinks for a moment about a distant land
called love
smiles to herself

knowing he'll be back next week
to worship at the temple

Rawene

low sky low sky low sky
moist clouds moist clouds
embrace embrace embrace
the hills the hills the hills
the inlet the inlet the inlet
laps at laps at laps at
the shore the shore the shore

startled birds

the sky flecked
with the flight of birds
in a moment gone

clouds sail over the horizon

we do not stay, we come and go

like startled birds
and drifting clouds

we are

we laugh we dance
we sing we fight
we love squabble and squawk
we hunt and are hunted
we dream and fly across the sky
we are birds

my whenua

my whenua lies buried at the Karori dump
beneath asbestos dirty nappies and waste
my mother lies in Karori cemetery
they'll probably run a motorway through her bones
if I'd died as a child they'd have taken my heart without asking
pickled it and put it on display in their library
our urupa has been turned into a sewage-disposal unit
there are oxidation ponds
where once we caught the kokopu
don't be a stirrer I'm told
excuse me if I piss in your cup of tea

In view of the fact hospitals are meant to be places of healing,
I say, 'Long live Irihapeti Ramsden.'

close

we picnic on the edge
of turbulent waters

close to the Hokianga Heads

we laugh and talk

'plenty have drowned
out there,' you say

the shoreline between
life and death

is slender and thin

unforeseen waves rise
they hiss and suck

whirlpools and eddies
twist and twirl by

haka

when i hear the haka
i feel it in my bones
and in my wairua
the call of my tipuna
flashes like lightning
up and down my spine
it makes my eyes roll
and my tongue flick
it is the dance
of earth and sky
the rising sun
and the earth shaking
it is the first breath of life
eeeee aaa ha haaa

the worm

the worm rises from
the mud, grows taller
than the sky

sprouts the head
of a jackal, a crocodile
and laughs like
a hyena

it trumpets justice
and chokes
the oppressed

it demands our adoration
is offended
when we refuse to bow to it

it is deaf and blind

it sniffs our corpses
gluts itself on our young

and grows fat with numbers

it devours all

it burrows into
the hearts of the blind
whence it rises again

Coca-Cola Jesus and Mitsubishi Mary

(Christmas in the Park, Christchurch, 2003)

we sit in the night and sing
'Glory to the newborn king'

beneath a plastic star
before the tinsel tree

a new car is sacrificed on the altar
who will win the keys to heaven?

wreathed with television angels
the prophets preach

'Silent night, holy night
Kolynos keeps your teeth white'

Jesus teaches, 'Things go better with Coke'

Mary rides a brand-new Mitsubishi
whose motor runs on virgin oil

MERRY XMAS FROM COCA-COLA

tangiwai

tangiwai weeping water
weeping water tangi
water tangi weeping
tangi weeping wai
weeping wai water
wai water weeping
water weeping waitangi
weeping waiting tangiwai
waitangi tangiwai weeping

poem for a princess

once from the chiefly line
from the seed of the rangatira

there grew the most beautiful flower in all of Waikato

her petals rivaled Tama-nui-te-ra in splendour

she hauled her tribe from the jaws of Hine-nui-te-po
she lived her life for her people, never for herself

therein lies her strength and beauty

on the banks of the Waikato River
all the taniwha call her name

Princess Te Puea, Te Puea Herangi

he piko he taniwha Waikato taniwha rau

dole-day warrior

so drunk
you can't stand on your feet
you beat your woman
you're afraid of work
you can't crawl to the toilet
without having a joint
you've traded the mighty moko
of your tipuna
for a jail tat
you're a thieving rat
every Friday and Saturday night
you play the tom-toms
on people's faces
with fists of fury
that's your only answer
you're a frightened little boy
you're a dole-day warrior
you flex your muscles
skite about your patch
your time in the can
six years for rape
oh wow what a man

e Api e
(in honour of Sir Apirana Ngata)

unmoving
like Hikurangi
you stood before the tides
that would sweep us away

your blood
like the people of Waiapu
flowed in your veins
like the river

your deeds made you
as tall as our mountain
the first mountain to catch
the morning light

you felled all who
stood against you
with your taiaha of mana and might

may we never forget your words
'E tipu e rea'
grow and stretch forth

aue aue, e Api e

harakeke

harakeke

'tis the flax
that adorns my land

harakeke

'tis black seed on brown stalks
proffered to the wind

harakeke

flax fingers
weave the moonlight

harakeke

promise of kete and basket

harakeke

'tis the muka
strands that tell our stories

harakeke

the rope that binds us

harakeke

'tis te pa harakeke
the people of the village
te rito o te harakeke

'tis the young shoot
the child

the centre
the heart of the plant

from which
our future grows
harakeke

to Te Rerenga Wairua

on the road to te Rerenga Wairua
dust billows from beneath the tourist bus
as it hurries by to the leaping-off place of the spirits

it almost flattens me, choking me with carbon monoxide
smothering me with dust
as i walk the path of our tipuna

i can't hear the sea, because of the chug a chug chug
of the bus's motor and the rolling rrrs
of American argot

'i gotta get me some of that dirt Sam,'

back into the bus they clamber
and are off in a puff of dust and smoke
having seen little

not knowing to wait in silence, with patience
then you understand the meaning of the word mana

then you see our dead gathering like clouds in the sky
slipping quietly from the tree into the sea

and you farewell them with love
and tears like the falling rain

it is

listen
it is
tree growing
flower
sowing
bird
talking
wind
blowing
rain falling
earth drinking
time
it is
feet
pattering
people
talking
sky
walking
time
it is
season
turning
leaves
burning
time
sun
warming
night
moon
chasing
day
time
gathering
time
it is
it is it is
time

time (1)

a forest of trees with leaves
`t`t`t`t`t`t`t`t`t`t`t`t`t`t`t`

a forest of trees without leaves
t t t t t t t t t t t t t t t t t t t t t t t t t

time (2)

wind-blown trees
`\`\`\`\`\`\`\`\`\`\`\`

lose their leaves
\ \ \ \ \ \ \ \ \ \

time (3)

an old man passing through the forest

o o o o o o o o o o o o o o o o o o o o o o o o
/) /) /) /) /) /) /) /) /) /) /) /) /) /) /) /)
\ / \ / \ / \ / \ / \ / \ / \ / \ / \ / \ /\ / \ /\

thought

a black and grey trout
in a black and grey stream

defined by light

swimming through darkness

struck

te mangoroa
is the long shark
known as the Milky Way

patiki is the flounder
another constellation of stars

i'm struck with awe and delight
when i see these marvels

for the long shark has been swimming
for millions of years
through the galaxy

and patiki the flounder
waits forever in the night's tidal estuaries

invisible

a brown leaf falls
onto a carpet
of matted leaves

an invisible thread
stitches the colours of the earth
into a pattern

of brown yellow and red
stitched into a blanket
of green lawn

a great seamstress

flying fish thread themselves
into the sea

a flock of gulls stitches itself
across the horizon

blanket stitching the earth and sky
together

God's a great seamstress
and painter

working on the ever-changing tapestry
of night and day

with colours threading
the weave of the sun's rays amid the clouds

the sky with the blanket of the sea
and the rich fields of corn

with textures of the moon

Swiss mountains

it's snowing on top
of the mountains
the snow will melt away

it's snowing on top
of my head a blizzard
that's here to stay

i'm going grey

survivor

I've learnt to rejoice
over my grey silvering hair
most of my friends are dead
Annie drowned in her vomit
from too many booze and pill cocktails
Punch hung himself in jail with his sheet
James pumped too much hammer
into his blue-rivered veins
cousin Wheels went the same way on his
birthday
a dirty needle poisoned Henry
a bullet cut Gavin down
a knife done Tawhai in
he bled his life away
Miro drove his car under a bus
anger and a baseball bat
smashed Leicester's skull wide open
Simon strung himself up in a cupboard
Dan fell asleep in the paddock
and got run over
by his drunken mates
Pete simply died
none of them got to thirty
life hangs on a slender thread
both weak and strong die young
only the lucky survive

stone age

we stand on the banks of the Danube

I'm a Ngati Porou Maori
my mate is Cheyenne

There's a nuclear reactor
on the other side of the river

we think of Chernobyl, nuclear reactors, radioactive leaks
uranium-coated shells

'i wonder if there's any fish in there,' i say
'if the fish glow in the dark don't eat em,' he replies

'i will dance to Ruaumoko the earthquake god,' I say

'ho,' he replies, 'i will dance the sundance'

'to life,' we smile

we dance on the eve of destruction

the sun sinks behind the silhouette of the dead city
and the moon is blood-red

aroha

aroha
aroha
aroha
aroha
aroha
aroha
aroha
aroha
aroha
aroha
aroha
aroha
aroha
aroha
aroha
aroha
aroha
aroha
aroha
aroha
aroha
aroha
aroha
aroha
aroha
aroha
aroha
aroha
aroha

the heavenly miracle
(for Pru)

the quiet sea began to hiss
the waves to toss and tumble
applauding the heavenly miracle

in the starlit heavens we saw
the first blush of light flood the sky
red beams and rays danced through the Milky Way
more subtle than any laser show

such beauty is only seen
once in our lifetime
it was the Aurora australis

God was dancing in the South Pole
and walking across the sky

autumn (1)

trees
dressed in
patchwork
coats

autumn (2)
(Christchurch, 2002)

the mighty painter is at work
turning the leaves from green to red
with dabs of paint

stripping away the old life
to make room for the new

old lives lie scattered on the ground
they will return anew
and clothe the tree in finery once more

blood drops
(Italy, 2003)

after much talk of war
she said

tutti hanno proprie
orgini ma dobbiamo
imparare ad amarci

we all have our origins
but we must learn
to love each other

Luciana sings
Sam is seed
Liliana sings

the sea is full tide
in Auro's eyes

cold wind strums my guitar

blood drops

piu pioggia
more rain

the Sami

have you heard the Sami sing
when they sing
their ancestors dance
across the sky
the northern lights flood the heavens
night lasts half a year
the day is six months long
reindeer stop to listen
such is the power
of Sami song

Written while on tour in Italy with Sami poets

the bellow

the bellow of the bull
the call of the ram
the song of the wind
earth and fire
the sharp knife
the bandit on the hill
a mother makes cheese
for her blind son
his mind sings songs
of Sardinia

He Dog

see the feather behind
the stars
the eyes behind
the bars

redskin ha!

behind Old Glory
there sits a man
with the sun dancing
in his mind

Written after seeing a photo of He Dog, the Lakota
Sioux, with the Stars and Stripes superimposed
over his image so he looked as if he were sitting in
a prison and the stripes were bars

warriors of love

we dance in the monster's mouth
we sing on the tip of its tongue
we embrace the teeth of adversity
we laugh before the red-raw throat of destruction
we fear not death
we thirst for battle
we are killers

dragons

beneath a canopy of blossom trees
an Asian student dances this way and that

in the shadows and light
she stoops to gather pink and white petals

that fall like snow
she presses them into her book

old wind blows her exam papers homework and notes
into the air they disappear over the Southern Alps

and she simply darts about gathering each delicate petal
no bigger than her thumbnail

she will imprint these flowers in her heart
when they are dry paper-thin blots of colour

she'll give them to her friend or lover
tell the world there's hope

she's remembered for a time what's important and what's not
as we file our teeth, arm for war and destruction

and the battle dragons come to drink our blood
in a cold blind world, slow to see the beauty of colour

and quick to forget

the bomber
(suicide bomber, Middle East, 2002)

carrying the bloody egg
taking everyone
for one last ride
leaving a hole
ribboned with guts and torsos
she dresses for the kill
announces her protest against oppression
and the slaughter of her tribe
with a bang
and a puff of smoke
eighteen summers old
she's happy to pay the price
of a ticket to death
with madness and hate
equal to that
of her oppressors

R.I.P.

rest in peace

rip

Easter eggs

they went off
over Easter
eggs
wrapped in hate
chocolate bombs
carefully laid
by another kind of Easter Bunny
born of oppression
they blew up
with a bang
instantly sped
and exited
the children
from life to death

as we searched
for the way
and prayed
for a new life
to come

six million

'Oh Api'

my friend Wolfgang weeps
as we walk up the road to Dachau
'You are proud of your ancestors
how can i be proud of mine?
my father was a Nazi
we fought over the dinner table
we've not spoken for years'

tears flood from Wolfgang's eyes

'I've never been able to visit the camps
i've lived here all my life'

brother Wolfgang weeps

his karanga to the dead rises
into the dull grey sky

the spirits listen in silence

as we walk up the road
on the corpses of six million dead Jews

peace lanterns
(Christchurch, 2002)

on the dark river
children's hands set peace lanterns afloat

a flotilla of lighted candles
drifts downstream

a puff of wind
blows them under the bridge

their spirits drift amid
the reflection of stars

in memory of Hiroshima
in memory of Nagasaki

the American eagle lays the first killer eggs

peace lanterns

in the east
green-lawned cemeteries
acres of Allied graves
speak in silence for those butchered in the camps

peace lanterns

with iron blood and bone
our tipuna stopped the Nazis

Hitler sent six million Jews
Poles dissidents homosexuals and children

for an early gas shower

they could have lived
to laugh under the sun and love in the night

if we'd shot the Führer
before he turned on the taps

shshshshshshshshshshshshshsh

peace lanterns

in the wind

by night
i've seen
the melody
of leaves

bathed in
the moonlight

i've heard
you whisper

in the wind

passing
through
the trees

in the city's din
and roar
of cars

i've heard
in the haiku
of morning

three leaves
falling

enveloped
in silence
whispering

psst
psst
psst

there is
another
way
brother

there is
there is
there is

Charteris Bay
(for Dennis Walker)

the day opened into a beautiful poem

tufts of clouds dissolved
on jagged hills

the inlet turned
the languid colour of pea green soup

lunch flowered into
fine wine salad talk and t'ai chi

the troubled mind sought
a t'ai chi pill
the instant hit of satisfaction

'observe take your time'
said the hills and sky

a wine-red stain seeped slowly
across the sea

the day closed
diamonds of sunlight danced across the water

the mauri
(for Pat Hammond and Sue McCauley)

she dices the onions
'You should have seen the sky' she says
turning with a smile

'it was something mate'
he says rolling a smoke

'the sky was orange
and so many colours'

we have a beer
smoke and talk
as we fill our glasses

Ranginui wears a cloak
of many colours

the mauri is all around us

rules

rain falls on a platinum sea

Pete's sister died

his tears fall in a world

that frowns on such emotion

'shshshsh, don't say a word,
forget it is the unspoken rule

we share a beer

listen to the game

his sorrow rises and falls

on the shores of Hine-nui-te-po

comfort

the korero
of my dead
mother

walls of the night

in our whare tipuna

woven into the stars
old black and white photos hang

we have placed them amid
the firmaments

uncle Tamati, cousin Hoera
Mum

death divides us

Roimata Toroa
tears of the albatross fall down the walls of the night

Golden Bay

silently waves break
on the dark edge

louder than
eternal night

is the chirrup
of a single cricket

teardrop

today

Lake Tutira
looks like
a teardrop

squeezed
out of the eye
of God

painter

i drink
colour

paint the world

with
my tongue

te ata kura

oh tender
shoot of peace
fragile leaf
tiny bud
on slender
stem
shine and grow
before
the red-tipped dawn
of war

Darts

words are
paltry things

so I turn them
into darts

and give them
wings

a sprig of beech

tiny lime green leaves
delicate tissue white
flowers a sprig of
beech wood have
i pressed into my
book of demons
let the colors
leach into the
pages and
quell their
bloody
thirst

cold

winter
breeze

trees
shiver

all saints day

he lights the candles
the names are called

in memory of the dead

she remembers
her friend and lover

tears fall from her eyes

two women wrap her
in their arms

beyond the mountains
deeper than the sea

the way is found within

Written at St Ninian's, Christchurch, 2003

senyru

1

'students don't talk
for one hour!' result
sixty minutes of mouse whispers

2

such power
he spoke to the masses
put them to sleep in five minutes

3

i pray for God's gift
to descend from heaven
a bird shits on my head

little tea cups

Kelly told me

'shetland pony hooves
look like
little tea cups'

then thought i

about ponies and horses

when a horse trots by

clip clop clip clop
clip clop clip clop

it goes

then it comes to a stop
raises its tail
and drops

plip plop plip plop
plip plop plip plop plippity plop

the swamp

there is no peace in the swamp
the mighty applaud themselves
the frogs begin to croak
eels emerge from holes
in the muddy banks
to bathe in the moonlight
and snap at the wayward moth
the fat rat weasel stoat and slinky cat
are on the hunt
mother duck loses six fluffy chicks
the ruru sees it all
rising in the night the mozzies bite

the wolf

the wolf howls
when the moon is full
and your blood is cold
she lopes along the mountain tops
hungry for a feed
she races the wind
through the valley of shadows
to you huddled by your fire
afraid of the cold night
gather up the last
of the old dead wood
to keep the flames alive
she sits on the edge and waits
when the fire dies
she leaps out of the darkness
and rips out your throat

the feral cat

the feral cat is a wild cat
patchy lean and mean
he slinks along in the shadows
pounces on the mouse in the forest
stalks the city rat
he's tawny with cat eyes
he licks his paws and purrs
after the kill
he is beaten
only by the bird in flight

the dream is real

the moon is an open eye
high in the sky or winking
at the world below
the wind is the sea's breath
rustling the leaves in the trees
night is a dark river
flowing through the day
a bird is a song
the dream is real
clouds are ghosts
flight is a wing

kete

1
kete

the galaxy
is the stars
fallen from
Tane's basket

2
stars

gypsophila
flowers
in a dark
bowl

3
fate

the stars are
God's dice
rolled
over the night sky

4
whanau

stars
a myriad
of children
sparkling
in the night

5

s

the s shaped eel
swallows the o
moon

6

0

the moon

looks at herself
in the water
mirror

free

the fluttering moth
circles the lightbulb

then breaks away

free at last

pepetuna

pepetuna pepetuna
kehua kakariki
wairua o te po
moe koe i te awatea
oho koe i te po
papaki mai ou parirau
rerere ai

prrrrrrrrrrrrr

oh moth
spirit of the night
you sleep by day
arise in the night
flap your wings
fly away

prrrrrrrrrrrrrr

the rose of peace

i have plucked
the rose of peace
before the raindrops
pelt the petals
to the ground
and the flood
washes it away

a line dropped from heaven

attracted to the lure
i take the bait
on a line dropped from heaven
wriggling and flapping
i'm hauled from the deep
to drown in the air
i'm a fish on a hook

jetty in the night

slap suck slap suck
slap slap suck waves lap
slap slap lap lap
around the jetty
in the night

stance

seagulls carry the sun
across the sky

offshore breeze

east breathes in
yin

onshore rain
yan

west blows out

4 lingual poem

wa
va
wa
va
i
si
api

Written in Maori, Samoan, Italian and English

what i am

adroit songster

natty dresser

attired in tuxedo

with immaculate cravat

i am a tui

words

sometimes words
blow through each other
like winds blowing
through the lines
of a poem
scattering   words

    all over
the   page

like   this

rat a tat tat

rat a tat tat

who's that knocking

rat a tat tat
rat a tat tat

it's machine-gun Johnny

chatter chat chat
chatter chat chat

sweeping the field

rat a tat tat
rat a tat tat

looking for the boy in a man-sized hat

for a chatter chat chat
chatter chat chat

for empire adventure and all that

rat a tat tat
rat a tat tat

the bullets spat
from the nostrils of the gun

rat a tat tat
rat a tat tat

mothers weep
there lies your son

rat a tat tat
rat a tat tat

16 years old
fancy that

rat a tat tat
rat a tat tat

freedom's not cheap

rat a tat tat
rat a tat tat

do we remember

chatter chat chat
rat a tat tat

who's that knocking

rat a tat tat
chatter chat chat

water

waves
lap about the rock

my mind
is washed away

questioning

a bud falls
before its time

i dig the garden

and wonder why

catching the waka

where the hell are you going

same place as you

yeah . . . but what the hell are you doing
on this waka

well . . . i don't know
i just got my ticket and got put on here

yeah . . . but what the heck are you doing here
look around . . . can't you see . . .
we've all got brown skin
and you've got . . . white skin

what difference does that make

we're all Maori and you're . . . one of them . . .
dare I say it . . . a Pakeha

well you know . . . we're all one
they just put me on here

well someone's screwed up
there's only Maori allowed on this waka
we're all going to Hawaiki
so you can't come
you're supposed to go to heaven or
dare i say it . . . that other place

well what can I do
i just paid my money and got put on
well you've gotta go
can't you see my tipuna will roast you
when we get to Hawaiki . . .
so . . . bugger off

oh I'm sorry you can't
unless you've got a parachute
we no longer go to Hawaiki in those
dinky little Maori waka
this is an aeroplane
we fly a la air Aotearoa
mind you we do things a lot better than those ... huas
no dry crackers and a glass of water here
no you get puha and pork bones
and as much beer as you can drink

ooh look ... there's God
that fellow out there with the long white beard
driving the sheep across the sky playing his harp
surrounded by all those
lovely little pink cherry bums
you better call out to God maybe he can help you ...
alas you're too late
Gods five hundred miles away ... goodbye God ...

you'll just have to hope for the best
let me tell you up front in first class
are all the Nga Puhis
we don't talk to them

soon those lovely little Te Arawa puhis
will come wiggling their bums down the aisle singing
'haere mai, haere mai, haere mai,'

we're Ngati Porou we have the back seats
we control the wharepakus
that makes us very powerful

you know how the saying goes
that lovely little Maori whakatauki
'we're the best stuff the rest

zzzzzzzzzzzzzz

147

hell typical Pakeha typical
i'm giving her the low down
and she falls asleep
oh well not my problem

oh we're so beautifully beautifully brown
like a lovely little batch of chocolate cookies
and we're so very very Polynesian
because being Maori is so absolutely super

i think i'll talk to those stunningly tanned beautiful
relations of mine across the aisle

tena koutou kei te aha koe
hello how are you

tofa sofua
fa'a fetai lava

Samoans

oh Jesus

can u c

can u c
u can c
c u can

fisherman's platter

'foods great but I can't stand all the flies,' says the diner,
'don't winge,' says the waitress,
'they're free, fresh and in season.'

animal

you may say
i'm not human
i'd say you're right
my heart is the wolf
my song is the whale song
my claw is the leopard
my call is the lion's roar
my home is the tiger's jungle
my den is the lair of the bear
my eyes are the falcon
my flight is the eagle

you may say i'm an animal
i'd say that's true
i've a tail
i'm croc's jaw
owl's feather
and bat wing
my bellow roars
from the balls of the bull
the lioness on the hunt

come dance with me tonight
between the horns of the moon
on the lonely plain
in the acid rain
in the blood-red sea

hear me

boooooaaaaaaggghhh

(to Pru)

let me write to you
of koru patterns
scrolls of fern

an island
a waka

we are on that
canoe sailing gently through
the lagoon

Pru

love we did

Pru's answer: love we do

O sun
(to Kiwa)

my gentle boy

stands on his own feet

as any warrior

Daughter
(to Jessie)

a beautiful
gift

Reremoana
(my daughter the sea spray)

a bird flies south
to Te Wai Pounamu
returns
with greenstone
in
her heart

Growing
(to Mihi)

my youngest daughter
was a delicate whisper

now she's
a gazelle

stepping across the living room
onto the plain

flight

my niece sets the table
she's singing

like a sparrow now
she flits from the table

across the sea
and grey sky

sipping

hovering above the horizon
a helicopter wasps about
sipping sunset's nectar
from night's black flower

time to leave

over the rim of my pint
i survey the world
the delicatessen across the road
the greengrocer's
everyone is struggling

this life mid-afternoon people
how they rush by

my jug is full
my cup's half empty

this place once filthy
with cigarette butts rugger
the races and pool
where Tania smiled and drank
where we crowded the table with plastic jugs
rattling the gats
happily guzzling our lives away

it's empty now, not a soul at the bar but me
the place is so clean
the music hypogenically homogenised piped and sterile

the barman haunts the bar

no smoking no drinkin
not a soul to be seen

no one's at the inn

it's time to leave

atea

atea
space

vast empty

empty

poem to Hone Tuwhare

the master

adroit composer of

'No Ordinary Sun'

has gone

and still

the music grows flows
grumbles and laughs

from his pen

only the old house has fallen
to the wind and storm

death shakes the tree
but the bird lives on

Thoughts before the headstone 08

we were just four artists travelling
in the north reading to the people

i stood before the A-shaped tombstone

HENRY WILLIAMS
the words said

the great man himself

i was drawn to the resting place of
his bones

i'd been out early in the morning walking

the waves broke about in Paihia
as they must've done when

the man himself was seen running about the place
with a piece of paper in his hand

before racing off down the path to ... Waitangi

tufts of grass grow and sprout out of the
headstone's temples

the wind blows over everything

we go our good works live on we're told

in the meantime

motels mushroom up all around the bay

you can't see the ocean because of the Tuscan villas and

flash eateries, you can get Mexican turtles in your soup
and Amazonian vegan burgers from Italy but . . .

the locals can't pay the rates

well what would you make of it oh sir

is this what it was all about

rates and property

laid to rest here with your support team of rangatira
sandwiched in between THE OASIS and
the HOLIDAY INN
with the high-rise CONTINENTAL
towering over you!

DEVELOPERS ARE LINING UP to
buy the very spot.

they'll probably shift your bones for a buck

that tells you how some treat history around here
not worth a scrap of paper eh

and JUSTICE

well that too

takoto mai ra i te poho o te atua matua me te
manaakitanga o te runga rawa

WAITANGI

WAITANGI
NO MATTER HOW MANY TIMES
YOU GO THERE

YOU'LL NEVER GET THERE
UNLESS YOU GO THERE
IN YOUR MIND

as if asleep

as if asleep

she lay

on the traffic island
stretched out

her long dark hair

a trail in the gutter

her young daughter behind her
gazing down with a gentle look

rocking the pram

looking at her mum

to whom Hine-nui-te-po had just come and called

'Haere mai ra sister,'

there she lay
as if in sleep

before the mall in Whangarei

Tiki tiki

tiki tiki
tiki tiki

but there's hardly anybody there

tiki tiki
it's just a marae
and horses
man

a few scattered people there
gallopin off
down the road

tiki tiki
a hundred

but there's nobody there

tiki tiki
tiki tiki

lost em all over there

in the war
Maori Battalion?

tiki tiki
tiki tiki

but there's hardly anybody there
just a few scattered kaenga

hell no wonder they call it
the greedy river

the Waiapu

i mean

Tiki tiki means a chief's topknot. It is also the
name of a tiny village on the east coast of the
North Island near the Waiapu River.

forever

ake ake ake tonu atu
forever and forever and
forever ake ake tonu
atu ake ake
ake tonu atu for
ever . . .

whew

thewind
chasedall
mywords
awaywhat
followsis
allihave
lefttosay